D1809059

A BELIEVER'S HEART

Barbara Klein

Bonita,
   Your prayers and
encouragement mean so
much to me.
   May my new little book
be a blessing to you.
            love,
               Barbara

A Believer's Heart
ISBN: 978-0-88144-530-5
Copyright © 2010 by Barbara Klein

Published by
Thorncrown Publishing Group
9731 East 54th Street
Tulsa, OK 74146
www.thorncrownpublishing.com

Printed in the United States. All rights reserved under International Copyright Law.
Cover and/or contents may not be reproduced in any manner without the express written consent of the author.

A BELIEVER'S HEART

A believer never thinks of his heart
Except as that place where God dwells
And so he guards and protects it
From doubt, fear and worldly squalls

As the calm in the depth of the ocean
As the beauty of a sunset at sea
As the sparkling of a rare diamond
Its wonder is exquisite to see

This heart once was darkened
But now is flooded with light
It lives in the love of the Savior
And daily is filled with delight

THE PATH OF
THE RIGHTEOUS

The path of the righteous
    is an ever-growing light
It proceeds from glory to glory
    and conquers in quiet might

This path is a great highway
    that leads ultimately to God's throne
It abounds in countless blessings
    that all come from Him alone

Don't seek this path in the world
    From it, it is fully set apart
Seek it only in the Lord
    for it's found in a believer's heart

REFERENCE:

Proverbs 4:18; II Corinthians 3:18; Psalm 84:5

REFLECTION:

Have you discovered the path in your heart?

RESPONSE:

Is there an area in your life where you are looking
too much to the world instead of to God?

A CENTRAL TRUTH

I wrap my heart around a central truth
That now I belong to Him
This means I've surrendered all I am
And all I've ever been

My life now lies before me
Filled with vistas to explore
It is He alone who leads me
And He who is the Door

REFERENCE:

John 10:7

REFLECTION:

How settled are you in your knowing
that you are eternally His?

RESPONSE:

Can you tell the Lord now just how much
you want to follow Him?

THE ARK

God told Israel to make a box
    called the ark of the covenant
Into it were placed the stones
    on which were the Ten Commandments

The ark was placed in the tabernacle
    in the most holy place of all
Above it the Presence of God shined
    and reminded Israel of His law

Since Jesus came and died and rose
    the ark is needed no longer
It's been replaced by a wholly other
    in which God's Presence is even stronger

This ark is new and pure and right
    with God's law written in its every part
It's filled with the joy of a full salvation
    for it's none other than the believer's heart

REFERENCE:

Exodus 25:10–22; Hebrews 8:10

REFLECTION:

Have you considered the spiritual significance
to you of the ark of the covenant?

RESPONSE:

Would your doing a study of the Old Testament tabernacle
and the ark help you in understanding better how
God wants to work in your heart?

I BELIEVE

I believe that You love me
And that I matter to You
I believe that You've saved me
And made me completely new

My life has taken on new direction
I'm doing things I never dreamed to do
I'm learning love, faith and obedience
I'll be Your work of art when I'm through

So help me to share with others
This simple life that sets men free
To face exciting challenges
And find sweet victory

REFERENCE:

Ephesians 2:10; I Peter 3:15

REFLECTION:

What effect does what you believe have upon your daily life?

RESPONSE:

With whom can you share what you believe today?

THE BRIDE

The heavenly Bridegroom
Is not satisfied with angels
Though multitudes
They may be

He is looking for His bride
His dove, His only one
Whom He has died
to set free

She is spotless, free of wrinkle
And without sin or stain
Her heart rests secure and centered
Until her Beloved comes again

REFERENCE:

Song of Solomon 4:9; 6:9; Ephesians 5:27

REFLECTION:

How secure is your love in your heavenly Bridegroom?

RESPONSE:

Could you pray now for Jesus to reveal Himself to you in your heart as your heavenly Bridegroom?

WHAT'S IMPORTANT

It's important to remember
Important things we need
To know

It's important to forget
All the things that we need
To let go

God is our best example
When we're tempted to settle
A score

He chooses to forgive and forget
And our sins He remembers
No more

REFERENCE:

Ephesians 4:32; Hebrews 8:12

REFLECTION:

*Is there something you need to remember or
something you need to forget today?*

RESPONSE:

*Can you by faith and obedience to God's Word now forgive
and forget any wrong or hurt that is still in your heart?*

THE FUTURE

The future is coming soon
And so I must be ready
I hear Your voice speak in my heart
"Fear not" though adversities be many

"Just keep looking straight on
not to the left or right
for I go on before you.
Walk by faith and not by sight."

So I hearken to Your voice
And Your peace I feel within
I know You'll never leave me
And will complete all that You begin

REFERENCE:

Lamentations 3:57; Philippians 1:6

REFLECTION:

Is there something about your future that concerns you today?

RESPONSE:

Can you make a decision now to stand on God's promise

in His Word to take care of you in your future?

GROUND

God created man of the dust of the ground
Ground's purpose is to receive seed
So the heart of man is the seed-plot
Of all that he will ever be

In the world man receives all the seeds
Of fear and doubt and hate
But when he receives the Savior
His heart is renewed ere it's too late

Now in his heart he begins to plant
The precious seed of God's holy Word
And his heart becomes a garden
As he lives out what he's heard

In this garden begin to grow
Faith and hope and love
The ground now rich and fruitful
Fulfilling the initial plan from above

REFERENCE:

Genesis 2:7; Luke 8:11

REFLECTION:

What kind of seeds have been growing up in your heart?

RESPONSE:

What seed of God's Word do you need

to plant in your heart today?

PEACEFUL WATERS

"Let not your heart be troubled."
   our Lord lovingly teaches
Let it be a calm, quiet pool
    that to the deepest depth reaches

Troubled waters make waves
    turbulent and restless
Peaceful waters make a mirror
    only serene and breathless

When our Lord looks upon your heart
    if it's troubled He only sees
The choppy waves surging
    driven by a very rough breeze

If your heart is not troubled
    being still and resting in His grace
Then as the Lord looks upon it
    He sees the reflection of His face

REFERENCE:

John 14:1

REFLECTION:

What does the Lord see when He looks upon your heart today?

RESPONSE:

Do you need to be still in His Presence and let Him calm
your troubled waters?

TIME, ENERGY AND MONEY

Time, energy and money
    three important commodities
and how I use them determines
    whether I'm a slave or free

They are meant to be my servants
    and I their master in control
living under my Master
    the Ruler and Protector of my soul

Day by day I must learn
    wise decisions with them to make
then find balance, joy and peace
    when I use them for His sake

REFERENCE:

Psalm 31:15; Psalm 100:2; Malachi 3:10–11

REFLECTION:

How do your personal values and your priorities
line up with God's Word?

RESPONSE:

What decisions and changes in these areas
do you need to make in order to enjoy
balance, joy and peace?

GOD IN ME

God wants me to know in Christ's love
    that I can be filled with the fullness of God
for any vessel when it's full is in essence
    full no matter if it's big or small

So it's not that my heart is vast enough
    to contain all the fullness of God
but that God is vast enough to dwell
    in my heart and fill it with His all

REFERENCE:

Ephesians 3:17–19

REFLECTION:

What does "the fullness of God" mean to you?

RESPONSE:

How can you respond today to God's desire

to fill your heart?

THE GARDEN

In the beginning God made a garden
    which was the center of the earth
In it was life and abundance
    where peace and joy were birthed

God made it for His man
    as a place for him to live
God wanted him to extend it
    and to the whole earth its life give

But, man sinned against God
    and this garden sadly was lost
But, God still had His plan
    for which He paid a very great cost

Jesus brought the garden once again
    into the life of the believing soul
Now it grows in the heart of each one
    whom Jesus has made new and whole

REFERENCE:

Genesis 2:8; John 3:16

REFLECTION:

What does it mean to you that your heart is God's garden?

RESPONSE:

What can you do today to extend your garden
out into the world in which you live?

A TREASURE

Once a man found a treasure
   quietly hidden in a field
He gave all he had to own it
   and to it his life did yield

A treasure has also been hidden
   from man's very first start
It lies waiting for his finding
   in the quiet depths of his heart

REFERENCE:

Matthew 13:44; Proverbs 21:20

REFLECTION:

Do you know what God has deposited in your heart and life?

RESPONSE:

How important is it to you that you find your true value?

Are you willing to take the time to find out what it is?

AFTER GOD CREATED ADAM

After God created Adam
    He put him into a deep sleep
and from his side God fashioned Eve
    then gave her to him in love to keep

She was made of his own nature
    made with him to reign
which is a beautiful picture
    of what God did when Christ came

Jesus endured the sleep of death
    and from His wounded side
each one who believes in Him
    God fashions as His bride

She is made of His own nature
    made with Him to reign
which becomes a beautiful reality
    when Christ Jesus comes again

REFERENCE:

Genesis 2:21–22; I John 3:2

REFLECTION:

What does being a member of the church mean to you?

RESPONSE:

How can you express your love for Christ today?

GOD'S GIFT

Many are the gifts
God has to give
Life and love and joy

They come from His grace
Freely given, never needing
Any of our employ

Each morning they come
Fresh as the dew
Like the singing of the lark

In sunshine and rain
The nicest of all
Is the gift of a grateful heart

REFERENCE:

Ephesians 5:20, Colossians 3:17

REFLECTION:

Is gratitude an inherent part of your character?

RESPONSE:

For what can you be grateful today?

THE PRICE

There is a price to pay
    to keep His Presence
And to hear His gentle whisper
    and know His sweet fragrance

It is the words you speak
    the thoughts you think
    the feelings in your soul

All must be captured
    and each moment surrendered
    if you would have His whole

REFERENCE:

II Corinthians 10:5

REFLECTION:

Are you willing to pay this price?

RESPONSE:

What thoughts or words do you need to bring captive today?

GOD IS WORKING

I rejoice! I rejoice!
For God is working in my heart
He shines His light, His love, His joy
Into every hidden part

He lets me know that He holds
My life in His tender hands
I am a child running in a meadow
Knowing my Father's plan is grand

REFERENCE:

Jeremiah 29:11

REFLECTION:

Can you rejoice today about what God is doing in your life?

RESPONSE:

Can you take some time to think about what it means
that God has your life and future in His hands?

PILGRIMS

As forlorn pilgrims
    we all wander through this earth
Never realizing our purpose
    never knowing our true worth

Then a great moment happens
    when we encounter the risen Christ
And our heart finds its deepest longing
    and we enter into life

Then we embark upon a pilgrimage
    very wonderful to behold
Filled with workings in our spirit
    that are more dear to us than gold

Now we journey toward a prize
    that's more precious than life itself
And we press on to receive it
    for it's none other than He Himself

REFERENCE:

I Peter 2:11; Philippians 3:14

REFLECTION:

What kind of a pilgrimage are you on now?

RESPONSE:

Do you need to adjust your priorities in order
to press on to your prize?

A SECRET PLACE

The Lord has a secret place
 It's the garden of His bride
There they enjoy sweet communion
 And she in His love abides

Fragrances sweet and pure
 Are there in rare delight
Life and love and light reign
 And there is never any night

They walk and speak in whispers
 And sometimes there are no words at all
Only a pure understanding
 And an eagerness for His call

There is found the banqueting house
 Overflowing with a very rich fare
There His voice is the joy of her heart
 And she's lost from all worldly care

REFERENCE:

Song of Solomon 1:12; 2:4, 8; 5:1

REFLECTION:

Do you ever take time to just be alone with Jesus and let Him speak to your heart?

RESPONSE:

Can you find a time and place today
to get alone and still your heart to listen
for the voice of your heavenly Bridegroom?

WHAT TO DO?

It's our most precious possession
    yet its so easy to lose
It can be absolutely firm
    yet become so hurt and confused

If we're not true to ourselves
    it will surely be led astray
And when we think we're doing just fine
    it will falter and give us away

What to do for this dilemma
    is to make a brand new start
And heed God's pleading call
    "My son, give Me your heart."

RFERENCE:

Proverbs 23:26

REFLECTION:

What would it mean to you to give God your heart?

RESPONSE:

What of yourself are you able to give God today?

MEASUREMENTS

The dimensions of Noah's ark
    in the Bible are clearly set forth
Also the tabernacle in the desert
    its east, west, south and north

So also is Solomon's temple
    as well as Ezekiel's temple vision
And finally are stated the dimensions
    of the New Jerusalem that is in heaven

All of these various measurements
    are descriptions of the household of God
Yet a greater strength is needed
    to apprehend God's spiritual measuring rod

This is the breadth, length, height and depth
    of the holy temple in the Lord
In which all believers everywhere
    grounded in love, their Lord adore

REFERENCE:

Genesis 6:14–15; Exodus 27:9–18; I Kings 6:1–10;
Ezekiel 40:1–42:20; Revelation 21:9–17;
Ephesians 2:21–22; Ephesians 3:17–18

REFLECTION:

*Have you come to know that as a believer
you are a part of the holy temple in the Lord?
Can you imagine just how big this temple is?*

RESPONSE:

*What does this understanding do for your
realizing and relating to the worldwide church?
Does it affect your tangible expressions of love
for your brothers and sisters in the Lord?*

LIGHT

It's the fastest thing on earth
Yet the simplest to behold
It enables us to find our way
Drives out fear and makes us bold

It comes with the sun each morning
And puts us to bed at night
Yet the most important thing it does
Is give a human heart its sight

REFERENCE:

Luke 11:36; Ephesians 1:18; Psalms 119:130

REFLECTION:

*Have you thought about the written Word of God
as spiritual light?*

RESPONSE:

*How can you welcome this spiritual light
more and more into your heart?*

PHILOSOPHY

Truth does not stand
In "I think therefore I am"

Truth lies in this
I am because God is

REFERENCE:

Colossians 2:8

REFLECTION:

Is your personal philosophy of life based more on
man's opinion or on God's Word, the Bible?

RESPONSE:

Do you need to make a realignment of your life's philosophy?

WORDS

Pleasant words
What a joy they are to hear

Affirming words
How they bring us love and cheer

Hopeful words
When heard they fill us to the brim

Helpful words
Just what we need when we're out on a limb

It's so important good words to say
What kind of words are you saying today?

REFERENCE:

Proverbs 16:24

REFLECTION:

Have you ever thought about the power of your words to impact people?

RESPONSE:

To whom can you say something nice today?

BELIEVING

Believing is the doorway
    that all God's gifts to you come through
Before you can receive anything from Him
    you must believe it's His will for you

Faith takes energy
    but then, so do doubt and fear
So why not use yours to believe
    you will receive all that to you is dear

REFERENCE:

Mark 11:23

REFLECTION:

What takes up more of your energy: fear or faith?

RESPONSE:

What decision do you need to make today
that will bring more faith into your life?

BLESSED

At the close of your life
    what's the best that men could say
About the way that you lived
    and filled up every day?

Will it be that you were rich
    or more famous than the rest
Or will it be the observation
    that they saw that you were blessed?

REFERENCE:

Numbers 6:23–26; Galatians 3:14

REFLECTION:

Have you considered what is involved in having God's blessing on your life?

RESPONSE:

Can you ask God today for His blessing to be more greatly manifested in your life so that you might be a greater blessing to others?

STAYING STEADY IN GOD

Staying steady in God
When the world is in a whirl
Rooted and grounded
Having found the precious pearl

Built upon the rock
Ready when the winds blow
Standing on His Word
Above the ebb and flow

Finding a deep peace
In the center of the storm
Life takes on its meaning
And faith takes on form

REFERENCE:

Colossians 2:7; Matthew 13:45–46; Matthew 7:24–25

REFLECTION:

How solid is your Christian life?

RESPONSE:

What decisions can you make now that will establish you
deeply in God's Word and strengthen your faith?

A MESSAGE

The grandeur of a Swiss mountain
The serenity of a Finnish lake
The beauty of an Austrian meadow
It took a great God to make

The wonder of a flower in blossom
The silence of an owl in flight
The joy of a rippling brook
All speak to a depth in my life

Nature carries a message
Its essence is good and true
It reveals the heart of the Creator
And fills mine with peace all through

REFERENCE:

Psalm 104

REFLECTION:

Do you enjoy nature?

RESPONSE:

*Could you take a walk today in a park or just look
outside at trees or flowers or some natural creation
and let it minister to your heart?*

THE SOUND

In the garden of Eden
    the first Day of the Lord occurred
and at the sound of God's Presence
    Adam fled from what he heard

Later on Mt. Sinai
    Israel would come to hear the sound
as the mountain trembled at His Presence
    and His glory shown around

Then on the day of Pentecost
    came the sound as a mighty wind
as the believers were all gathered
    His Presence filled them all within

Soon a great Day is coming
    when the Lord descends from heaven
and takes His own up with Him
    while the sound again is given

At this moment all is quiet
    waiting for you to make a start
and respond now to His making
    the sound of a knock at your heart

REFERENCE:

Genesis 3:8; Exodus 19:16; Acts 2:2; I Thessalonians 4:16;
Revelation 3:20

REFLECTION:

*Have you responded to God's "sound" for salvation
and for the infilling of the Spirit?*

RESPONSE:

What response do you need to make to God right now?

FETCHED

Samuel came to the house of Jesse
    prepared to anoint a king
All the older sons were presented
    but only the youngest received the calling

So Samuel fetched David
    and poured the oil on his head
Out of the cold and into the fellowship
    David was sovereignly led

Years later king David would fetch
    Mephibosheth out of fear and loneliness
And give him a seat at his table
    for he remembered how it was to be fetched

Every born-again child of the King
    in his heart has a moment deeply etched
Of when he entered heaven's royalty
    because he was sought out and fetched

REFERENCE:

I Samuel 16:1; I Samuel 16:13; II Samuel 9:5

REFLECTION:

*The Old Testament gives us pictures of what in the
New Testament is a spiritual reality.
Have you been born again?*

RESPONSE:

*If you know about Jesus or maybe you are religious,
but you have never been born again and now you
would like to once and for all by faith receive Jesus
into your heart, please pray with all your heart
the prayer on the next page.*

A PRAYER TO PRAY TO BE BORN AGAIN

Lord Jesus, I believe in my heart that You are the Son of God. I believe that You died on the Cross for my sins and that You rose from the dead. Come into my heart. I receive You now by faith as my Savior, and from this moment on I make You the Lord of my life. Thank you for saving me. Amen.

Copies of this book may be acquired at
www.overflowingwells.com

LaVergne, TN USA
02 June 2010
184622LV00004B/62/P

9 780881 445305